Manga Touch

Jacqueline Pearce

Orca currents

ORCA BOOK PUBLISHERS

Library and Archives Canada Cataloguing in Publication
Pearce, Jacqueline, 1962-

Manga touch / written by Jacqueline Pearce.

(Orca currents)
ISBN 978-1-55143-748-4 (bound)
ISBN 978-1-55143-746-0 (pbk.)

I. Title. II. Series.

PS8581.E26M35 2007 jC813'.6 C2007-903835-2

Summary: The manga touch is everywhere in Japan,
but Dana still feels alone.

First published in the United States, 2007
Library of Congress Control Number: 2007930411

Orca Book Publishers gratefully acknowledges the support for its publishing
programs provided by the following agencies: the Government of Canada
through the Book Publishing Industry Development Program and the
Canada Council for the Arts, and the Province of British Columbia
through the BC Arts Council and the Book Publishing Tax Credit.

Cover design: Teresa Bubela
Cover photography: Getty Images

Drawing of author: Nina Matsumoto

Orca Book Publishers
PO Box 5626, Station B
Victoria, BC Canada
V8R 6S4

Orca Book Publishers
PO Box 468
Custer, WA USA
98240-0468

www.orcabook.com
Printed and bound in Canada.
Printed on 100% PCW recycled paper.

010 09 08 07 • 4 3 2 1

For my daughter, Danielle

Acknowledgments

This book couldn't have been written without the help of others. I'm enormously grateful to my good friend, Jean-Pierre Antonio, who has lived in Japan for over seventeen years, was a great host during my visit to Japan and continued to answer questions via e-mail and phone calls throughout the writing of the book. I would also like to thank the many people in Japan who showed me kindness and hospitality, especially Kyoko Nishihara, Masako Nakai, Kikumi Tanaka, Takako Horri, Taeko Kobayashi, Aisling Braiden, Michiko Kihira, Sakano-san and the Ito family. Thank you also to Sheya Eno, who shared her experiences as a Canadian exchange student in Japan; to Tomoyo Ihaya who read over some scenes in the book; to the students at Iino Highschool in Suzuka-shi, who answered questions about Japanese student life; and to everyone else (both in Japan and Canada) who answered questions, talked with me about manga, and otherwise offered support and encouragement. And finally, I would like to acknowledge the artful word-cutting skills of my editor, Melanie Jeffs.

chapter one

I stare out the window as the airplane taxis down the runway. With my back to the other seats, I can almost forget I have to share my two weeks in Japan with Melissa Muller and the others. The Melly Mob, I call them. If you've ever seen a gang of crows mob some poor raven, you can figure out why.

Melissa and her friends flock together like crows. If they don't like you or your clothes or your hair color—pomegranate red, being my latest—they don't exactly dive-bomb you. But they have a way of looking at you that says you rate about the same as bird crap.

A thrill leaps through me as we lift off. We rise into the clouds, and Vancouver disappears. I'm glad to see it go. Outside there is nothing but whiteness. It feels like I'm in a magic passageway between worlds. At the other end of all this whiteness is a different place.

I turn away from the window and glance around the inside of the plane. I don't know the girl beside me other than her name, Maya Contina. She's talking across the aisle to a friend. Ignoring me. A couple of rows back, Melissa is sitting beside her boyfriend, Zach Bellows. Their heads are bent together. Someone throws a scrunched-up piece of paper at them. Zach laughs and throws the paper back. Melissa pretends to be annoyed, but it's obvious she likes the attention. She is wearing even more makeup than usual. I am wearing a lot of black eyeliner myself but only because I want to look different. Melissa looks like she's trying to be some kind of phony fashion model. All her clothes are name brand, and she keeps flipping her long blond hair off her shoulders.

Melissa's eyes snap onto mine as if she's sensed me. I give her a bored look. She looks away. For a second, I'd swear she almost squirmed. A bit of the old Mel showing through? I turn forward again. Nah. There is nothing left of the Mel that used to be my best friend.

The seat belt sign is off now, and I pull my backpack out from under the seat. I take out my MP3 player and my sketchbook, flip open the book and begin to draw.

With light pencil strokes, I sketch the shape of a body and face. I draw over the lines more heavily as I get them the way I want. I draw manga-style eyes—but not too large. I add two sections of hair that sweep off the girl's face like raven wings.

As I lean over the sketchbook, my own hair falls like a red curtain around my face. I am in my own world. But I can feel the others noticing me and pretending they don't.

Maybe I'll fit in better in Japan. At least I know about manga and anime—Japanese graphic novels and animation. I've been a fan since the first episode of *Sailor Moon* that I saw as a kid. I quickly discovered other stuff after that and went from TV shows to manga books. The character I'm drawing now is influenced by the darker manga I've been into lately.

Woosh! The sketchbook flies out of my hand.

"Let's see what you're working on, *Red*," a boy's voice says.

"Hey!" I twist around, yanking my earbuds loose. I come face to face with DJ, the most annoying guy in our school. Just my luck to be seated right in front of him.

"My *name* is Dana," I tell him with a knife-edge glare.

I grab for the book, and DJ holds it out of my reach, laughing. I want to slap the taunting grin off his face.

"It speaks! It speaks!" he says. He's lucky my hands can't reach his throat.

"Give me the book," I order under my breath. By now everyone is watching. Everyone except for Mr. Crawford and Ms. Delucci, our teachers. They are busy ignoring the morons they are supposed to be watching.

I make another lunge for the book, and DJ jerks it away again. Unfortunately for him, there's not much space in an airplane seat. I grab a handful of his hair.

He gives a sort of squeal. It is part surprised pain and part laughter. Then he tosses the book. The next thing I know, my sketchbook is in the hands of Zach Bellows. He starts flipping through the pages.

I force myself not to scream, though I am bursting with anger. For a second, I catch Melissa's eye and glare. If she has any memory of our friendship at all, she knows how much I hate people looking at my private drawings.

Mustering extreme willpower, I turn away and sit down. If I pretend I don't care about the book, they should lose interest. Unless they start making fun of the drawings. I feel a surge of panic.

"Here, pass this over," a girl's voice whispers from the aisle.

The next thing I know, Maya drops the sketchbook into my lap.

"What did you do that for?" DJerk complains.

I look past Maya to see Melissa making her way back to her own seat.

"The movie's about to start," she says, giving him a flirty smile. "It'll be hard to watch with you guys throwing stuff around."

chapter two

"We are beginning our descent," the captain's voice announces. "We will land at Nagoya airport in thirty minutes."

Finally! This is it. We are closing in on a patchwork of small green and brown fields. It's getting dark, so I can barely make out the colors. Alongside the fields are the gray shapes of buildings.

Disappointment nudges through me. I

guess I expected the clouds to part and everything below to dazzle like jewels. But the view is dull and gray and no different from Vancouver.

It's just the weather and the fading light, I tell myself. It'll get better.

Inside the airport, we could be anywhere. There are just as many English signs as there are Japanese ones. I step onto a moving walkway as a recorded female voice says "please watch your step" in perfect English. The voice also says something in Japanese that must mean the same thing. We pass through customs and head to the baggage claim.

By now, I'm watching for a washroom. I see a sign with the English word toilet. On one door is a small blue man-shaped image. On the other door is a small, pink, woman image. I push open the pink door and step inside. I'm followed by a couple of other girls from our group. The washroom is clean and modern. I open the door to the first empty stall and freeze.

For a second, I wonder if I picked the wrong washroom. I'm staring at a men's urinal, but it's on the floor. It's a Japanese-style toilet, I realize. Now I feel like I'm in a different place.

"What the hell is that?" a familiar voice complains.

I look over my shoulder. Melissa is standing in front of a stall, one hand on her hip.

"You stand over it and squat," I say. Then I step into my own stall as if I know exactly what I'm doing.

The look on Melissa's face is worth the price of this whole trip.

"Well, that's it. I'm holding it," I hear Melissa say. I am still laughing to myself as I reach the baggage claim area.

In the airport lobby, a Japanese man in a black suit introduces himself as Mr. Akimoto. He is our host teacher from Suzuka High School. He has a round face lit by a welcoming smile. His thick black hair fits him like a tight hat.

We follow Mr. Akimoto out of the

airport, pulling our suitcases behind us. I look around, hungry for my first glimpse of Japan. But it's dark out now. I can't see much past the concrete of the airport. It's warm, though, and more humid than spring in Vancouver. I take a deep breath of Japanese air.

"Aren't we getting taxis?" Melissa asks.

As he leads us toward a covered walkway Mr. Akimoto explains that the airport is built on an artificial island. We have to take a ferry across Ise Bay to get to Suzuka. I squint, trying to make out the lights on the other side of the dark bay. All I can see are a few fuzzy spots that aren't quite as black.

A tall, sleek, white boat pulls in to the dock, and we walk on. The interior of the ferry is super modern—bright lights, airplane-style seats, TVs hanging from the ceiling. I feel a sense of unreality as I sink into my comfortable chair. Fatigue hits me. It's about three in the morning Canada-time, I realize. I have been awake for nineteen hours.

We get off the ferry at a place called Tsu. I notice a few short palm trees, which I wasn't expecting. Several teenage boys are skateboarding in the parking lot. We look over at them with interest. Mr. Akimoto guides us to a waiting bus.

We board through the back door. As we struggle to find space for all of our suitcases, I look out at the skateboarders. Dressed in loose T-shirts and slouchy pants, they could be kids anywhere. One boy with spiky black hair reminds me of a manga character—the cocky, rebellious hero type. I feel a tingle of anticipation. What will my host family be like? Will I meet someone like that manga boy?

The bus drives on the left side of the road, which is a bit unnerving. The streets seem darker than back home. There are large signs everywhere with Japanese writing. No English now. The bus pulls up in front of a train station, and we file out of the front door. Mr. Akimoto pays for us as we leave.

"Everything here is backward," Melissa complains.

"Yeah," Zach agrees with a laugh.

My hackles rise. Was Melissa always this anal?

"Maybe it's you that's backward," I say. Melissa and several of the others turn and stare at me. Then their eyes glaze over as if I'm not here.

"Did you hear something?" Melissa says to the girl beside her.

The girl shrugs. "No, just a weird buzzing sound. Street noise, I guess."

They turn their backs on me—as if I care.

On the train, I notice an ad with a manga-style illustration of a woman's face. Cool. Mr. Akimoto tells us that we will be in Suzuka in twenty minutes. We will meet our host families at the station. I clutch my backpack tightly, feeling my stomach begin to flutter. I'm not sure if I'm nervous or just excited. Soon I will be rid of Melissa and the others—at least for a while.

chapter three

"Welcome to Japan. My name is Fumiko Seto."

My host "sister" steps forward. She has a shy smile and a heart-shaped face. Her black hair is cut in a fashionable shoulder-length style. She is wearing her school uniform. The other Japanese kids are also wearing uniforms. The boys' black pants and collarless jackets look military. The girls' plaid skirts, black blazers and white blouses look like Canadian private school uniforms. Suzuka High is a public school, though. Compared to the Japanese kids we look pretty grubby and travel worn. Except for Melissa, who must have touched up her makeup and hair.

"This is my mother and father," Fumiko tells me, gesturing toward the man and woman standing beside her. Her English is good, which is a relief.

"Hi," I say, forgetting that I'd planned to say *konbanwa,* Japanese for good evening.

My host mom and dad smile and bow. Then they take turns shaking my hand. I can tell that they don't understand much English. But they seem friendly and kind. Mr. Seto is not much taller than me, and his hair is threaded with gray. Mrs. Seto is shorter than me. Her face is an older version of Fumiko's. Mr. Seto picks up my suitcase and says something in Japanese. I figure it means follow me, please.

"I am sorry my older brother, Kenji, could not come to the train station," Fumiko says as we follow her dad.

"That's okay," I say. I'm curious and a bit nervous about this older brother.

As we reach the doors I look back at the rest of the kids from my school. They have all split off with their host families. A stab of panic shoots through me, but I shove it aside. I'm glad to be getting away from them.

"*Sayonora*, suckers!" I say under my breath.

Ahead of me Melissa moves through the doors. She glances over her shoulder. For a second, her eyes look like a scared little kid's. Then she notices me and glares.

The Setos usher me out to a boxy van with Honda Stepwagon Spada written in English on the side.

"My father works for Honda," Fumiko says, sounding proud.

Mr. Seto gestures for me to get into the front of the car. There is an awkward moment when I try to climb into the driver's seat. I forgot that driving on the opposite side of the road means driving on the opposite side of the car. Eventually I make it into the passenger seat. I lean back, ready for sleep, but excitement and nerves keep my eyes open. Driving through shadowy unfamiliar streets with three strangers, I suddenly feel very far away from home.

We pull up to the Setos' house, which is crowded between other houses on one side of a narrow road. They all look pretty much like North American houses but not so large. Many of the roofs have curving eaves. Across the street is a black empty area, with more houses beyond that. As I climb out of the car, I hear odd creaking sounds coming from the blackness. I can't see what is out there.

Inside the Setos' house is a small entrance that is lower than the rest of the house. I take off my shoes, which I know you are supposed to do in Japan. Still, I get the feeling I have done something wrong. Mrs. Seto quickly sets a pair of blue cloth slippers on the upper level in front of me. Fumiko touches my arm.

"Like this," she says. She steps out of her shoes and right up to the next level and into a pair of slippers.

"The lower floor is for shoes only," she explains.

I am standing on the shoe-only floor with my socks.

"Oh, sorry!" I say. I jump into the slippers, feeling foolish.

Mrs. Seto holds out her hand as if I am a scared animal she is trying to calm. She gives me a confused smile. Fumiko laughs, covering her mouth with one hand.

"It's okay," Fumiko says. "Everyone forgets some time."

Who knew shoes would be such an issue?

Mr. and Mrs. Seto exchange words in Japanese, and a new voice joins in. I look up and meet the dark brown eyes of a shaggy-haired teenaged boy. He doesn't smile.

Fumiko introduces her brother, Kenji.

"I am happy to meet you," he says stiffly, like he's reciting from an English textbook.

A look passes between Fumiko and her mother, and there is an awkward silence. Then Fumiko touches my arm again.

"Come, please," she says. "I'll show you our house."

Her mother stalls her with a few words of Japanese.

"I'm sorry." Fumiko turns to me, looking embarrassed. "You must be tired. I should have asked if you want to go to your room."

This time it's Mr. Seto who cuts in.

"My father suggests you might be hungry," she says. "Would you like to eat?"

I glance from one attentive face to the other. Only Kenji hangs back, looking bored. Suddenly I feel overwhelmed. All I want to do is escape to a soft bed—or even a hard futon. A picture flashes into my mind of a Japanese wooden pillow I'd seen in a book. But at that moment I don't care what they give me to sleep on.

The house tour is postponed. Mrs. Seto excuses herself to prepare me a bath. I think I am about to learn that baths are different here too. After some urging by his father, Kenji picks up my suitcase. Fumiko and I follow him up a steep set of stairs. Kenji pushes open a door at the top landing and sets my suitcase down. I step into the room, relieved and a bit disappointed to see a short soft-looking bed. No futon on the floor and no wooden pillow.

I start to thank Kenji, but he is already gone. What's his problem? I wonder, but I'm too tired to think about it now.

Fumiko shows me the bathroom, which is steaming up from the hot water pouring into a deep tub. The floor is tiled, and there is a shower nozzle and hose attached to the wall beside the bathtub.

"Where's the toilet?" I ask.

"Down the hall," Fumiko explains. "In Japan the bath is separate. In the old days, people did not have a bath in their homes at all. They went to a bathhouse."

"That sounds kind of fun," I say.

Fumiko turns off the water. "There, it's ready now." Seeing my confused look, she adds, "You sit on the chair to wash first."

She points to a small plastic stool beside the tub. "Or stand and shower if you like. Then you can get into the bath and relax. Take as long as you like."

"Do you want me to empty the water out of the tub after?" I ask.

"No, my mother will drain it when we have all finished."

I get it now. You wash first to keep the water clean. It's like a hot tub, but with people taking turns instead of getting in all at once. Maybe in the old days they all bathed together in the bathhouse.

"I will say good night now," Fumiko says. "But if you need anything, please ask."

"Thanks," I tell her. "I'll be okay."

I lock the door behind Fumiko. It feels good to be alone.

When I step under the shower, I imagine I am washing away my old life. I lower myself into the steaming tub. I feel like I'm sinking into Japan and whatever comes next.

chapter four

I wake up feeling warm and cozy. I'm ready for my first day in Japan. I fling off the covers and jump out of bed. I pad barefoot to the window and push open the curtains.

Whoa! I am looking at a rice paddy. That's what the dark space was across the street. It's the size of a city block, flooded with water and surrounded by houses. The sun is beginning to rise over the rooftops.

Short tufts of green poke out of the water in dotted lines. A crow flaps lazily across the field and lands on a roof.

I'm not sure what I expected, but it is not to see a rice paddy in the middle of the city. Today should be interesting.

Now, what am I going to wear for my Japanese school debut? I choose a short lime green plaid kilt and a purple T-shirt. It clashes nicely with my hair. Not a look Melissa and her friends will love. At least I won't look like everyone else.

When I go downstairs for breakfast, Mr. Seto has already left for work. Fumiko, Kenji and I sit at a North American-style table. Mrs. Seto sets out boiled eggs in little cups, bowls of yogurt and thick slices of white bread. Again, it's not what I expected. I soon learn that this is the Setos' idea of a North American's breakfast.

"This is good," I tell Mrs. Seto through Fumiko. "But I'd like to try a Japanese breakfast while I'm here."

Mrs. Seto smiles and nods, looking pleased.

Across the table Kenji glowers. He pushes aside his yogurt and gets up, muttering in Japanese.

"He has to get to school early for soccer practice," Fumiko explains.

I wonder what he really said. Kenji seems like a jerk. But then he smiles at his mom and says something that must mean thanks for breakfast.

After breakfast, Fumiko gives me a tour of the house. It includes a special room that has *tatami* mats on the floor. They are made from some kind of grass. There's a little wooden alter by the far wall and a special alcove called a *tokonoma*. There is a vase of flowers on a shelf and a scroll painting in the alcove, but there are no other decorations in the room. We have to take our slippers off before stepping inside. Not even slippers are allowed on the *tatami* floor. Fumiko explains that in the old days this would have been a typical room in a Japanese house.

Fumiko also shows me her bedroom. It is small with a pink bedspread and matching pink curtains with frills. She has a tiny cluttered desk and posters of Japanese pop stars on the walls.

My eyes zero in on a colorful book on the desk.

"Is that manga?" I ask.

"Yes," Fumiko answers, her eyes lighting up. "Do you like manga?" She pronounces it *munga*.

"Some," I say, trying not to sound too excited. She pulls the book out from under the papers and hands it to me. The title is in Japanese. The cover shows an image of a girl with a large head and huge liquid-looking eyes.

"Do you have any other manga?" I ask. I try to keep the disappointment out of my voice. This looks like it is for little kids.

"Oh yes," Fumiko says, digging through the clutter on the desk.

She holds up another book. I recognize the blue cat on the cover. Doraemon, the robot cat from the future. More kid stuff.

"Do you have any *Full Metal Alchemist* or *Bleach*?" I ask.

"Ah, you know those manga?" she says, impressed.

"Yeah, we have them in Canada," I say.

"You like adventure manga?" she asks.

"I guess you could call it that."

"I like more...," she pauses, searching for the right English word, "...light-hearted manga."

"Oh." She likes the cutesy stuff with the big eyes.

"Kenji's favorite is sports manga. But he might have one of the kind you like," Fumiko says. "You could ask him after school."

"Sure," I say. Though I can't picture Kenji lending me something of his.

We hurry back downstairs. Fumiko explains that she usually takes the train to school, but this morning her mom will drive us. Mrs. Seto has packed our lunches in small plastic boxes. She gives me a lunch box wrapped in blue fabric.

Mrs. Seto drops us off outside the school gates. The gates will be closed when school starts, Fumiko explains.

"They lock you in?" I ask.

"Oh no," she says, her eyes wide. "Students can get in and out, but no cars can drive in."

The building is large and modern. We join the crowd of students walking and riding bikes into the grounds. Most of them look at me with interest. Mr. Akimoto, the teacher who met us at the airport, is standing by the school.

"*Ohayo gozaimasu, sensei,*" Fumiko greets him with a slight bow.

I copy her. I am not sure how to bow, so I omit that bit.

"Good morning, young ladies," Mr. Akimoto says, smiling broadly.

In the foyer everyone is switching from shoes to green plastic slippers. Fumiko finds slippers for me. We store our shoes in her cubbyhole. There are no lockers.

We are greeted by squeals of excitement in the hallway. A pack of Japanese girls rushes up to us. Fumiko's friends, obviously. Except for one slightly taller girl, they are all about the same size as Fumiko. I feel very large next to them.

Fumiko introduces me. The other girls are shy as they say hello. Then they turn back to each other and talk all at once. The shortest girl has a backpack with about twenty little plastic toys hanging from it. She says something that sounds like *kow-wah-ee*, in an excited voice.

The other girls look me over and nod.

"*Kawaii* means cute," Fumiko explains. "They think your outfit is cute."

Cute is not exactly what I was going for, but I smile and thank them.

"*Kow-wa*...," I try, not getting it right.

They all laugh and repeat the word.

"*Kawaii*," I say, pointing at the little toys dangling from the backpack. In the name of international relations, I give no sign that the toys make me want to gag. What is it with all this cute stuff?

"*Hai*," the girls agree in Japanese. They seem pleased with my efforts.

"Do you like shopping?" the shorter girl asks.

Shopping? What kind of question is that? I shrug.

"Sometimes, I guess."

"Yeah, shopping at Value Village," interjects a male English voice.

I turn to see DJ's mocking grin. He ducks as if expecting me to punch him.

"Is that a store in Canada?" Fumiko asks.

"Yeah, a store *he* can't afford to shop at," I say loudly after DJ's retreating back.

I follow Fumiko into her classroom. She finds an extra chair so I can sit beside her. The girls gather on one side of the classroom and the boys on the other. They don't mix like we do back home.

Fumiko's friends cluster around us, whispering. I get the feeling they are working up to asking me something. Finally the taller girl is pushed forward.

"Do you...?" she begins. She falters and turns to Fumiko.

Words fly around the group. The others seem to be urging Fumiko to ask the question now. She looks embarrassed.

"Do you dye your hair?" Fumiko finally asks.

I laugh. This is their big question? "Of course," I tell them. "My real color is light brown."

They all talk at once again. Fumiko tells me that students are not allowed to color their hair. The school has strict rules about personal appearance.

"What about that girl?" someone asks. She points across the room. A crowd has gathered around Melissa. Figures. Of course I get stuck in the same class as her.

"Does she dye hers?" Fumiko asks, her eyes on Melissa's pale blond mane.

I'm tempted to say yes, but I know that her hair has been that color since she was small.

"No, that's her real hair," I admit.

Fumiko's friends look impressed. At that moment, my eyes meet Melissa's.

They catch for only a second. Then she looks through me, as if I am invisible. I wish I had told Fumiko's friends that her hair is phony—just like the rest of her.

A loud student voice at the back of the room calls out some kind of command. The Japanese students immediately stand behind their desks. A teacher walks up to a podium at the front of the room and bows. The Japanese students bow back.

Homeroom lasts about five minutes. Next we have English class. Today the Canadian kids stand at the front of the room and answer questions: Do you like bands? Do you play basketball? Etcetera. Most of the students' English is not as good as Fumiko's. We have to speak very slowly.

There is a ten-minute break between classes to give the teacher time to move to the next class. The students stay in the same room. Math is next. I don't understand what the teacher is saying, but I can read the numbers on the board, so I can follow some of it. There are two more classes before lunch break. I am soon totally out of it and totally bored.

For lunch we stay in the classroom. Fumiko and her friends push their desks together, so that we can talk. I unknot the blue cloth around my lunch box, feeling like I'm unwrapping a present. The box is divided into compartments. The biggest one contains rice. On top of the rice is a pink thing that Fumiko says is pickled plum. There is also a piece of fish, some green beans—all cold—and a slice of apple. The apple is cut so that the peel looks like pointy rabbit ears. Very *kawaii*. Aside from the apple, it's the kind of meal I'm used to having hot, but it's pretty good.

After the lunch break Fumiko and her friends get ready for the next class. I stand up and look for the rest of my group. Time for our tour of the city.

chapter five

Melissa and Zach lead the group out of
the school. She sticks to Zach's arm like
a leach, laughing her phony laugh. A bus
is waiting for us outside the gate. I climb
on and aim for the first empty seat.

"Sorry, this seat's saved," the girl sitting
by the window says.

"Whatever." I give the seat a look like I
wouldn't want to go near it anyway.

I continue down the aisle until I see a
pair of empty seats. I slump into one and

toss my backpack onto the other. Sorry, this seat's saved, I mouth to the back of the girl's head. Then I turn and stare out the window.

Thump. Someone bumps the back of my seat.

"Wha's up, Red?" asks an annoying voice.

I sink lower in my seat, ignoring DJ. God, it's like being back on the airplane.

"Can I have your attention, people?" Ms. Delucci's voice rises thinly through the din.

"Excuse me!" she tries again. But no one is listening.

Behind me, DJ is talking about some vending machines he discovered.

"Man, anyone can just walk up and buy a pack of cigarettes or a can of beer!" DJ says. His voice is filled with awe.

I roll my eyes. Whoever thought DJ would learn something on this trip must not know him.

Suddenly a piercing whistle cuts through the noise. The talking stops and all eyes turn forward. I sit up straight and see that Mr. Crawford has pushed up behind Ms. Delucci. Behind him stands Mr. Akimoto, who is either embarrassed or very interested in a dust speck on the floor. I wonder if he's thinking how poorly behaved we are.

"All right, now that I have your attention," Mr. Crawford says. He gestures for Ms. Delucci to continue.

"I want you all to remember that you are ambassadors for Canada while you're here," she says. "That means you must be on your best behavior."

She pauses and stares sternly at us. I feel like she is looking right at me. Then I realize the look is meant for DJ.

"Now," she continues, "Suzuka High School and Mr. Akimoto have generously arranged a tour for us. Mr. Akimoto is giving up his afternoon to act as our guide."

She sweeps out her arms as if welcoming a performer onto a stage. Mr. Akimoto steps forward holding a cordless microphone.

A sudden blast of music booms through the bus. For a second I think Mr. Akimoto is going to burst into song. I notice several television screens hanging from the ceiling. Every screen, blank a second ago, is now filled with what looks like a Japanese music video. Japanese script scrolls across the bottom of the screens.

"Karaoke!" someone yells.

Mr. Akimoto fiddles with the controls. The music silences and the screens go black.

"I am so sorry," he apologizes with a bow. He sits down abruptly as the bus lurches into motion.

"As you can see," he says, "this bus is equipped for karaoke entertainment." He pronounces it *kar-a-Oh-kay*. "Perhaps you would like to try it later."

Several people cheer. Mr. Akimoto smiles tolerantly. Ms. Delucci and Mr. Crawford give us the evil eye.

"But first, I am very pleased to show you the city of Suzuka," Mr. Akimoto continues.

"Our first stop is the Suzuka Museum of Traditional Crafts, which specializes in *katagami*. This is the famous Japanese stencil art used to decorate the clothing of samurai," Mr. Akimoto tells us. There are a few sounds of interest at the word *samurai*. Mr. Akimoto mistakes this for general keenness. He goes on with enthusiasm.

"There were many *katagami* shops in this area in the old days. Travelers would stop to buy fabric on their way to the famous shrine of Ise."

Behind me, DJ and his friend snicker.

As the streets of Suzuka roll past us, Mr. Akimoto continues to talk. He points out the Honda factory and the new North American-style mall called Bell City. Apparently *Suzuka* means bell and deer. The name has something to do with a lost person and a bell hung from a deer's neck.

I try to ignore DJ, who is doing an imitation of Mr. Akimoto.

"And there you have the famous Japanese smokestack," DJ says as we drive by the

Honda factory. "And now you see the famous Japanese traffic sign..."

I want to tell him to shut up. But I have to smother a laugh when he points out "the famous pick-up-after-your-dog sign." The sign has a cute cartoon dog, which makes the meaning obvious.

Some of the stores we pass have signs with manga-style illustrations—mostly the big-eyed cute variety. I smile to myself. The manga touch is everywhere.

By the time we arrive at the craft museum, I am happy for a break from both DJ and Mr. Akimoto. The museum tour is interesting, but DJ and the others have the attention spans of gnats. While Mr. Akimoto translates the guide's explanation of stencil-cutting, I realize I am the only one left in the museum. Everyone else is either in the gift shop or back outside.

"How does that stay together?" someone asks.

I turn around, surprised to see Zach. He is bent over a large stencil covered with tiny detailed cuts. The museum guide explains how a thin mesh is added to the back of the stencil to hold it together. The dye goes through the holes in the stencil and through the mesh.

"The whole process," Mr. Akimoto concludes, "from preparing the stencil paper to cutting the stencil, can take two or three months."

And that's just for one stencil. Probably several stencils were used to decorate one piece of fabric. Not the kind of art I'd have patience for.

We join the others in the gift shop. Melissa grabs hold of Zach, throwing me a harsh look. I pretend not to notice.

After the craft museum, the bus takes us to a Buddhist temple and a Shinto shrine. Both are several hundred years old. Everything is interesting, but I'm getting tired of old things. What about all the modern stuff that Japan is famous for? Nintendo, state-of-the-art electronics, Tokyo clothing fashions, anime, manga...

As we climb back on the bus, people complain that the tour is boring. Maybe

Mr. Akimoto hears, because the next thing I know, we are driving by a racetrack.

"The famous Suzuka Circuit," Mr. Akimoto says, pointing out the window. I swear I can feel the bus tip as everyone leans in that direction. But our excitement is short-lived.

"We don't have time to stop there today," Mr. Crawford says. He waves away the groans of disappointment.

"Mr. Jung, please take your seat," he says to DJ, who has stood up in protest.

"What are we doing next, then?" DJ asks, a whine creeping into his voice. "When are we going to eat?"

"Yeah," a few voices join in. "I'm so hungry."

Mr. Crawford holds up his hands.

"What part did you not understand about being on your best behavior?" he says, letting his glare fall on each person in the bus. "Now, sit down and be quiet. No one's going to starve. Our next stop is dinner."

chapter six

In the restaurant, Mr. Akimoto tells us that a food buffet is called a *Viking* in Japan. Maybe the Japanese think Vikings eat this way. Whatever, the food looks great. There is a long counter covered with different things to choose from. The plates and bowls are smaller than the ones in restaurants at home. I heap different kinds of noodles, sushi, tempura and various mystery foods onto a plate.

Melissa and Zach are at one end of my table. As I walk by, I notice that Zach is trying just about everything, while Melissa only has a few small things on her plate.

I sit down and prepare to dig in. The waitress has given us forks as well as chopsticks. I pick up the chopsticks and start with some sushi.

A man sitting nearby picks up his bowl with one hand and uses chopsticks to scoop up long noodles. The noodles stretch between his mouth and the bowl. I can hear the slurp as he sucks up the noodles. This seems like a fun way to eat, so I try it with my own noodles.

"Gawd!"

I look up and see Melissa looking at me with disgust. How long has she been watching me? Staring right at her, I scoop up more noodles and suck them noisily into my mouth. She turns away with a huff. Zach laughs. He catches my eye for a second, nods his head in Melissa's direction and rolls his eyes.

That was weird.

After we have finished eating, we wait outside for our host parents. The Stepwagon pulls up with Mrs. Seto at the wheel. I'm disappointed that Fumiko isn't with her. Mrs. Seto tries to tell me something about Fumiko and Kenji. Since she doesn't have much English and I have no Japanese, it takes most of the drive for me to figure out that they are at a place called a *juku*. It has something to do with school.

When we arrive at the house it's starting to grow dark. Mr. Seto is kneeling on the front steps trimming the branches of a miniature tree in a pot. Several small potted trees are arranged up one side of the stairway. Mr. Seto stands up to greet us. We stop to admire the trees.

"Bonsai," Mr. Seto says, and I nod. I recognize the word.

"You make them small?" I ask.

"Small, yes." He nods. I'm not sure if he's agreeing they are small or if he's saying that yes, he's the one who prunes them.

Mrs. Seto opens the front door and holds her hand out, indicating I should enter first. A sound catches my attention, and I hesitate.

Creak, creak.

It's the same sound I heard when I arrived. It's coming from the flooded rice paddy across the street.

"*Kaeru*," Mr. Seto says, noticing my curiosity.

"Frogs?" I ask.

He nods and smiles.

"*Kaeru*. Frogs."

I grin back. It's a little thing, but it feels like a big breakthrough in communication.

"I want to take a look," I say, waving toward the other side of the street.

Mr. Seto's smile disappears, and he says something in rapid Japanese. It goes straight over my head. So much for the breakthrough.

I gesture toward the rice paddy again and take a step in that direction.

Mr. Seto sets down his clippers and follows me.

"I'm just going across the street," I try to tell him. But it's no good. I have an escort.

We walk the short distance in silence and stand at the edge of the field. It's almost dark now, but there is still a tinge of pink in the sky. The croaks have stopped. We stand stiffly, waiting for them to start again. I scan the edge of the water and the rows of green plants but see no sign of frogs.

"It's okay, we can go back," I say with a sigh, figuring Mr. Seto will understand.

"I guess going for a walk by myself is out of the question," I comment under my breath as we walk back to the house.

I hope Fumiko will be home soon. I feel out of place in the Setos' house without her. I can't talk with her parents, but they don't want me to be on my own. I try watching television with them but can't follow anything. I feel an overwhelming urge to speak to someone in English. I wonder what my family is doing right now. Of course it's the middle of the night there. They are all still sleeping. Maybe I should e-mail them and let them know I'm still alive.

The Setos understand me when I say I'd like to use the computer—*konpyuta*, as Mr. Seto says. Mr. Seto sets me up in Fumiko's room, switching her computer to English characters. I'm afraid he's going to stay in the room with me, but he leaves after I thank him.

I type a quick note: *The Setos are nice, the food is good, etc.* It's just the usual meaningless stuff that parents want to know. I'm just finishing when Fumiko and Kenji come home.

"Hi," Fumiko says when she finds me. "Did you have a good day?"

"Yeah, it was pretty good," I tell her. "You were getting tutored?"

"Tutored?" she asks. "Oh, you mean *juku*, cram school. I have much studying to do and get help there. So does Kenji. Do you have cram school in Canada?"

"Ah..." I have to think. "Not exactly. Last year I had a chemistry tutor for a while...someone who helped me study."

"You don't have help now?" she asks.

"No, I don't really need it anymore," I say.

"You must be a very good student," Fumiko says wistfully.

"I'm not that great a student," I tell her, "but I do okay."

"I see," she says, frowning. "In Japan, everyone who wants to go to university goes to *juku*. I am afraid I will not get into a good university if I do not study and do well on exams. Don't you want to go to university?"

"I guess. I haven't thought much about it yet. I'd like to study art, but maybe I'll do computer graphics or something."

"I want to be a translator," she says. "I want to translate English books into Japanese or work for a company with English clients." Her eyes meet mine for a moment with a look of intensity, and then they flick away. "But I don't know if my English will be good enough."

"It seems really good to me," I tell her. I'm surprised at how worried she is. I had pegged her for someone who avoided anything more serious than choosing which Hello Kitty barrette to wear.

Before bed, I have a hot bath again. It's a routine I could get used to. In my room afterward, I pick up my sketchbook and flip to the manga character I've been working on. She stands legs apart, arms across her chest as if she is blocking out the world. But she's daring it to come at her at the same time. I pick up my pencil and begin to sketch. She needs some kind of power, like a magic sword or a jewel pendant...

I start to sketch a sword hanging at her waist, but it doesn't seem right. I try a dagger instead...Maybe it should be something more futuristic—some kind of gun...no, that's not right, either...

I can't just come up with a character on her own. I need to figure out what kind of world she lives in. I try to imagine where my character is, who her enemies are. But I can't concentrate.

I toss the sketchbook onto the bed and sigh. Did Zach Bellows look at me like he was sharing a joke about Melissa tonight? Nah, that couldn't be right...I walk over to the window. Across the street, the rice paddy is dark. I can hear the frogs croaking.

So far, Japan is not what I expected. I feel like I have seen so much but just touched the surface. There is still a whole hidden world out there.

chapter seven

The next morning I ask Fumiko if I can borrow a couple of her manga books.

"Sure," she says, "but wouldn't you rather borrow some from Kenji?"

"No, that's okay," I say quickly. "I should give *Doraemon* a try."

We head down to breakfast. I have *Doraemon* and another manga under my arm.

"*Ohayo gozaimasu*," I say to Mrs. Seto.

Kenji is at the table eating what looks like miso soup. He's using his chopsticks to pick things out of the bowl.

"Hi," I say, sitting down and setting my books on the table beside me. Fumiko sits next to me.

Kenji looks up, grunts something and then goes back to eating. He is wearing a blue T-shirt under his uniform. I wonder if that's against the school rules.

On the table in front of me is a bowl of soup, a bowl of rice and a small dish with a piece of fish and something else. I pull my soup closer and look for a spoon, but there are only chopsticks. Out of the corner of my eye I see Kenji pick up his soup bowl and drink from it. I pick up my bowl and do the same.

"Is this a typical Japanese breakfast?" I ask.

"Yes," Fumiko says. She explains that the stuff with the fish is *natto*, fermented soya beans.

The pink plum I recognize from my lunch yesterday. I pick it up with my chopsticks and pop it in my mouth. Sour, but good.

I notice Kenjo sneak a look at me from under his bangs. His glance lingers on the manga beside me, but I can't read his expression.

We have less time to get ready for school this morning since we have to walk to the train station. Mrs. Seto hands me my lunch.

"*Arigato gosaimasu*," I tell her. Japanese words are starting to feel more natural.

We leave the house with Kenji, but as soon as we are out the door, another boy hails him. The boy is thin with longish hair. He pushes his hair away from his eyes to get a better look at me.

"Hi," he says carefully. "My name is Takeshi. What is your name?" He grins, pleased with himself.

His smile is infectious. I can't help smiling back.

"Hi, my name's Dana," I tell him.

He laughs and looks at Kenji as if it is hilarious that I answered. Like I'm a talking animal or something. This gets me annoyed.

"Hey, I'm still here," I snap. "And yes, I can talk."

He looks back surprised. Fumiko laughs, her hand over her mouth. Kenji scowls, but I ignore him. Takeshi grins at me again, and I smile back. He seems like the kind of guy you couldn't stay mad at for long.

"Hey, you've got a blue T-shirt on too," I say, seeing blue at his collar. "Isn't that against the school rules?"

He continues to smile, but he obviously hasn't a clue what I said. He turns to Kenji, who looks away. Fumiko translates.

"Ahh!" Takeshi's grin broadens. He stops walking and begins to unbutton his shirt. Kenji looks embarrassed.

"Japan soccer team!" Takeshi says. He opens his uniform shirt to show me a blue soccer jersey with a black and white crest. The crest is a crow with three legs. The center leg is kicking a soccer ball.

"Cool," I say.

"Cool," Takeshi repeats. "*Sugoi.*"

"*Sugoi* means cool?" I ask.

Takeshi nods and grins broadly.

"Why does the team crest have a three-legged crow?" I ask.

This time Takeshi turns to Fumiko right away. She translates my question. The two boys talk for a minute. Then Takeshi turns back to me and shrugs. Kenji looks away.

"I don't know, either," Fumiko says, embarrassed.

"That's okay," I say and change the subject. "So, they don't get in trouble for wearing a T-shirt under their uniforms?"

"They'll get in trouble if they don't button their shirts over top," Fumiko says.

Kenji is a few paces ahead of us now, and Takeshi hurries to catch up to him. Kenji and Takeshi walk on together, their backs to us. Takeshi turns around briefly to include us with a grin. If I'd thought Kenji's unfriendliness was a Japanese boy thing, Takeshi has proved that wrong. I step closer to Fumiko.

"Why doesn't Kenji like me?" I whisper.

Fumiko stops walking and looks at me with surprise. Then she looks down, embarrassed.

"Kenji likes you," she says, but she won't meet my eyes.

"He doesn't talk to me," I say.

"He thinks he can not speak English well. He does not want you to know," she whispers. This time she does meet my eyes.

"You're kidding?" My mouth drops open.

"No." She shakes her head. "It's true. It hurts his pride to admit his English is not good."

I want to ask her more, but the boys have stopped to wait for us.

As we catch up, Takeshi gives me a teasing smile.

"Girls talk so much, they forget to walk," he says, looking proud of his joke.

"Just giving you a chance to stop and admire us," I say. I give him my best mocking imitation of a flirty Melissa smile.

He laughs. He may not understand what I said, but he knows at least that I'm teasing him. Kenji has turned away and started to walk again, so I can't tell if he's cracked any hint of a smile. If he does like me, he's sure keeping it secret. Takeshi's English isn't very good, but it hasn't stopped him from being friendly.

We funnel into the small train station, joining the line up in front of the ticket machines. Fumiko buys our tickets, and we push through the turnstile. We don't wait for the boys. The platforms are crowded with kids in school uniforms and adults dressed for work. I don't see any other Canadian kids. I am the only person in the whole crowd with red hair. Several people sneak looks at me.

We manage to find seats on the train. Some people have to stand. Takeshi and Kenji squeeze in to stand in front of us. As the train starts, a couple of students nearby get up the courage to ask Fumiko and the boys about me. Soon all the kids on the train start to shift toward our end of the car. They call out questions and press close to listen. I feel like a celebrity—though Fumiko does most of the talking.

When we get off the train, we walk a few blocks to the school. Most of the train crowd is with us. I walk with Fumiko and the other girls. Kenji and Takeshi drift off with the guys. The girls press close, giggling and excited. One taller girl is encouraged to stretch to her full height next to me while the others compare us. The girl is still a couple of inches shorter than me. They all exclaim over how tall I am.

It's weird to have all these girls buzzing around me. I wonder if this is what it feels like to be part of the Melly Mob—to have everyone pay attention to you instead of pretending you don't exist.

chapter eight

As we approach the school, I find myself hoping Melissa and the others will see me. Me, being popular. But then I catch myself. How lame. I don't care what Melissa and her so-called friends think. Unlike her, I don't need a bunch of groupies hanging off me to feel good about myself.

A bus is already parked in front of the school, and Mr. Crawford and Ms. Delucci are standing in front of it.

Ms. Delucci waves me over. I say good-bye to Fumiko and the others.

"We're getting an earlier start on our tour today," Ms. Delucci tells me. "If you can help me round up the others, I'd appreciate it."

I look at her blankly. Me, *round up* the others? I don't think so. Interpreting my look correctly, Ms. Delucci sighs.

"Well, we'll have to wait until the homeroom teachers announce it, then," she says.

"We could always leave without the others," I suggest.

"Right," she says sarcastically. Then we catch sight of DJ and a couple of other boys. "Though it is tempting," she adds.

When our group has assembled beside the bus, Mr. Crawford holds up his hands for our attention. Before he can say anything, DJ calls out.

"Are we going to the racetrack today?"

"No, Derek, we are not going to the racetrack," Mr. Crawford says with forced patience. "You can do those things on your own time. Today we are going to a Japanese historical site."

There are a few groans.

"What kind of historical site?" Zach asks from near the front.

"We're going to visit an old town called Seki-cho," Mr. Crawford explains. "In the old days, Japan was ruled by the Shogun, the head of the samurai lords. He lived in Edo, which is now Tokyo. The emperor was only a figurehead then, and he lived in Kyoto. All the lords had to have homes in Edo as well as on their own land. They had to spend every second year in Edo, so the Shogun could keep control over them."

Mr. Crawford is in socials-teacher mode. "So, there was always a lot of traffic flowing to and from Edo. The main route between Kyoto and Edo was called the Tokaido Road. There were stations or rest stops all along the route. Seki-cho was one of those stops. It hasn't changed much in two hundred years."

"That's just great," Melissa grumbles. "I guess they don't have Starbucks or McDonald's, then."

A few people snicker.

"And we have one more surprise," Mr. Crawford continues. "Mr. Akimoto can't come with us today. He's making arrangements for a special trip tomorrow."

"Where? Where are we going?" Several interested voices interrupt.

"I'm not going to tell you until we know for sure," Mr. Crawford says. "I've got a cell phone with me, and Mr. Akimoto will call as soon as all of the plans have been confirmed."

He holds up his hand for attention as talk ripples through the group.

"Now, since Mr. Akimoto can't be with us, the school has decided to let its two top English students join us." He pauses to let this sink in. "Some of you will know them: Fumiko Seto and Aki Nishikawa."

I'm one of the first people on the bus this time. I find a seat near the front where Fumiko will see me. After about fifteen minutes, Fumiko and Aki show up. They climb on, and Ms. Delucci introduces them.

Fumiko looks pleased but shy as she smiles at all of us. She sees the empty seat beside me and gives me a grateful look when I gesture for her to join me. I feel weird to be actually saving a seat for someone.

"See," I whisper to Fumiko. "Even your school thinks you're a good translator."

Fumiko shakes her head and hides her smile behind one hand, but I can tell she is pumped.

The drive to Seki-cho takes about a half an hour. The bus lets us off in front of a temple.

Mr. Crawford gestures down the narrow street of wooden buildings. Many have curved roofs and wooden bars over the upper story windows.

"As I was telling you earlier," he says, "this street has hardly changed in over two hundred years. I'd like you to imagine for a minute what it would have looked like with the street full of samurais and ladies in kimonos..."

There's silence for a second as if everyone really is trying to picture it. Then Melissa's voice cuts through the quiet.

"Look, there's a café. It says in English right there on the sign."

Everyone turns to see.

"I'm dying for a coffee," she announces, like we all care. "Please tell me they have normal coffee."

She looks past Zach.

"Where's that girl?...Fumiko, you have to help me," she pleads, catching sight of Fumiko beside me.

Mr. Crawford holds up a hand to get our attention again.

"You're welcome to get a coffee if you like and explore the street on your own. But before you all take off, we need to go over a few things." He gives us a quick version of the you-are-ambassadors speech. Then he tells us to meet back at the temple in two hours.

Melissa pushes through the group and grabs Fumiko's arm.

"Come on, Fumiko," she says, ignoring me.

Fumiko turns and apologizes before allowing Melissa to drag her away.

"I will help people order coffee," she says to me and anyone listening. "Then we can walk along the street and look at some points of interest."

I watch Fumiko disappear into the café with Melissa and the others. So that's it. I've lost Fumiko. Was I thinking I was going to spend the day with her? Did I actually want to? Whatever. I'm not sticking around to hear Melissa dis me in front of her. There is a dull ache in the back of my chest, but I shove it aside. I'd rather be on my own anyway.

Maya and a few others are walking down the middle of the street just ahead of me. I stop and pretend interest in a shop window. In the window display a yellow ceramic cat sits with one paw raised as if beckoning people into the store. I hesitate for a second, take a deep breath, and then I push open the door and step inside.

The store is small and crowded with trinkets. An older woman wearing a faded pink apron over modern clothes stands behind the counter. She smiles and says something in Japanese. I smile back.

"I'm just looking," I say in English.

On one shelf there is a row of yellow cats, smaller versions of the one in the window. I pick one up and look at it. The cat has a red collar with a gold bell painted around its neck. On the bottom of the figure is a sticker that says five hundred. Five hundred yen is somewhere around five dollars.

"*Maneki-neko*," the shop woman says, coming out from behind the counter to hover beside me.

"Lucky cat," she adds in careful English.

I nod and smile. I've seen cats like this in Japanese restaurants back in Vancouver. This one looks handmade. Maybe my mom would like it for her office.

"I'll get this one," I say, bringing the cat to the counter.

The woman ducks behind the counter. She wraps the cat in tissue paper before placing it in a plastic bag. She says something in Japanese and pushes a tray across the counter toward me. I place a thousand yen bill onto the tray. The woman smiles broadly and sets my change into the tray. I smile back. It's like we're talking with smiles.

"*Arigato gozaimashita*," the woman says as I turn to go.

"*Arigato*," I tell her.

Back on the street again, I'm in a better mood. This is the first time I've been in a Japanese store by myself, I realize. It went pretty well. I need to get away on my own more on this trip.

The rest of the morning I duck in and out of stores, trying to avoid Melissa. This also means keeping out of sight of Fumiko. But I'm sure Melissa and the rest of the group are keeping her busy. At one point I see them a block away talking and laughing. Before they notice me, I slip through a doorway into some kind of museum.

A woman greets me in Japanese. When I don't understand, she hands me an English pamphlet that says the building used to be an inn. I pay the entrance fee and walk through a dirt passageway. The pamphlet explains what all the rooms used to be. This passage was the kitchen. There is a room at the front of the inn with a raised wooden floor where the inn's guests were greeted.

On the top floor is a sleeping room with old-fashioned futons on the floor. There are wooden headrests that look like pedestals with little flat pillows on top. I can't imagine how anyone could sleep on them. The inn has three separate sleeping rooms. The floor of each room is slightly higher than the last. Apparently, the more important the guests were, the higher their sleeping level. At the front of the inn, the windows that overlook the road have angled wooden bars in front of them. The pamphlet explains that the bars allowed people to look at the street below without being seen. Ordinary people were not supposed to look directly at higher class people. But if everyone knew what the bars were for, it would be no secret that they were being looked at, it seems to me.

Still, I like the idea of being able to spy on people down below. I look out through the bars to test it out.

I realize it is time to meet at the temple. I won't be able to avoid the others any-more. As I walk back up the street, I fix my face into a non-caring mask.

chapter nine

At the temple, I check in with Ms. Delluci
and Mr. Crawford. A few people are
already sitting on the stairs eating their
lunches. DJ and another guy are kicking
a hacky sack around in the middle of the
courtyard. I walk past them, ignoring the
comment DJ throws at me.

At the other end of the courtyard is a
shrine with a statue of a kneeling bald guy
inside. Someone has tied a cloth baby's

bib around the statue's neck. The bib is faded and weathered—like it's been there for a while.

Suddenly something thuds into the side of my head. I whirl around.

"Sorry about that, Red," DJ calls loudly. The hacky sack is lying on the ground at my feet.

"Yeah, right," I say under my breath.

"Can you throw it back?" he has the nerve to ask.

Not likely. I give him a look of disgust and turn away.

There is a little gate at the back of the courtyard. I walk through it, ignoring DJ. I follow a path that leads to a garden. There is a small pond in the middle of the garden and a narrow path winding around it. I find a bench behind a tree, sit down and take out my lunch. On the other side of the pond, low-hanging trees and shrubs flow down the hill like a waterfall. Maybe I'll take my sketchbook out after I eat. Maybe instead of working on my manga girl I'll try drawing the pond.

As I unwrap my lunch, I notice a ceramic frog with a baby frog on its back. Is that what the frogs in the rice paddies look like? Is it just decoration or does it mean something? There are so many things in Japan that are still a mystery to me. I don't know how I ever thought I would fit in here.

After lunch I am forced to head back. The bus is waiting at the temple. Reluctantly, I walk to the back of the group.

"Dana!"

I turn to see Fumiko making her way through the crowd. Behind her, Melissa looks annoyed.

"Are you okay?" Fumiko asks. "I was worried when I couldn't find you."

"Yeah, I'm fine," I say, a little snappier than I intend. What is it with her and her family? Why don't they want me to go anywhere on my own?

"Why didn't you wait for me?" she asks.

"You were busy translating," I say. It sounds like an accusation.

Fumiko stares at me for just a second.

She looks confused and maybe hurt. Then she looks down.

"Your friends asked a lot of questions," she says.

"They're not my friends," I tell her.

Fumiko and I climb onto the bus together, not talking. When the bus is full, Mr. Crawford raises a hand for our attention.

"I've just heard from Mr. Akimoto," he says. "Our special trip is a go."

"So, are you going to fill us in?" someone calls out.

He's probably discovered another museum or old town for us to visit, I think.

Mr. Crawford is smiling. "Tomorrow," he says, "we take the bullet train to Tokyo."

A cheer explodes through the bus. More questions are thrown at the teachers.

"How long do we get to stay there?"

"Do the host kids get to come?"

We are going for three days, including travel. Just the group from Canada, plus

Mr. Akimoto. My mind is jumping with images—like a crazy channel clicker. Tokyo. Tall buildings. Crowds of people. Manga studios. Modern stores. Lights. Signs. Everything.

I'm still lost in my imagination when Fumiko leans close to me.

"Have I done something wrong?" she asks.

"What?" I look at her, startled.

"Did I do something to make you angry?"

"Of course not," I say sharply. Then I catch myself. This is Fumiko I'm talking to, not Melissa and the rest.

"Look," I start again, making my voice softer. "I'm not mad at you. You didn't do anything wrong. It's just..."

How can I explain?

"I think I understand," she says quietly. "You said the others are not your friends... I think you are like Kenji."

"What do you mean?" I demand.

"When he fears embarrassment, he is like a nut—hard on the outside."

"I'm not embarrassed," I tell her.

"Maybe not," she says. "But maybe something else." She looks at me sideways as if she is checking the impact of her words.

I force myself to swallow the angry comeback that rises in my throat. I'm not anything like Kenji.

Back at the Setos' that night, I pack for the trip to Tokyo. I flip through the pages of Fumiko's *Doraemon* manga. I wonder if I should bother taking it. It is mostly filled with drawings of the boy, Nobita, and Doraemon, the oversized cat. The people's eyes are huge, and there are lots of exclamation marks coming off the faces to emphasize emotions. Doraemon pops out of a drawer, and Nobita is startled. Nobita eats an animal cracker and starts turning into a cat. Doraemon gets mad, more people get mad...But that's about as much as I can figure out.

There is a knock on my door. I open it and am surprised to see Kenji standing there. He holds something out to me without meeting my eyes. A pile of manga books.

"Thanks," I say as I take them. The one on the top is *Full Metal Alchemist*. Fumiko must have told him the type of manga I like.

We stand there for a second. Before I can think of anything to say, he walks away. I remember Fumiko saying that Kenji acts like a jerk to hide his embarrassment. Maybe it's true, and he's not so bad after all.

I close the door and sit on my bed, laughing to myself. I'm picturing a manga panel of me and Kenji looking at each other. Our emotions are drawn in *Doraemon* style. I look like Nobita when Doraemon climbs out of the drawer. My eyes bug out, my mouth opens wide. Lines of surprise shoot out around my head. Kenji has water drops of anxiety coming from his face or maybe crosshatched shading across his cheeks to show his embarrassment.

But if Fumiko is right about Kenji, is she also right about me?

chapter ten

In the morning we take the express train to Nagoya. The trip is about an hour and a half. We buy *bento* box lunches in the Nagoya station while we wait for the train to Tokyo. The streamlined, white, bullet trains ease in and out of the station almost silently.

Finally we board one with a long rounded nose. The train is already full of people, so we have to spread out. I slip into an empty seat beside a Japanese businessman, so I don't have to sit with anyone from our group. As the others settle into seats, Ms. Delucci walks up the aisle, counting heads and giving warnings. I sit back and dig into my cold *bento* box lunch. I stare past the man beside me and out the window. We soon leave the city behind. The train speeds through rolling farmland, rice paddies and clusters of houses with brown tile roofs. Occasionally I glimpse the ocean.

After about an hour and a half, Mr. Akimoto walks down the aisle, telling us to look out the windows on the left of the train. We may be able to see Mount Fuji, a sacred mountain. I'm on the opposite side of the train, so I have to look past the people across the aisle. I can't see much.

"I think I see it!" someone from our group calls out and is echoed by other voices, both English and Japanese.

A Japanese woman across the aisle steps out of her seat and gestures for me to take her spot so I can get a better view. I move over quickly, smile my thanks and bend to the window. There, now I see it. A brief glimpse of a white peak through a gap in the clouds.

"We're lucky today," Mr. Akimoto says with a broad smile. "Mount Fuji does not always show itself."

A few people point cameras out the window before the clouds swallow the mountain again. I return to my seat, thanking the woman once more. The businessman beside me smiles as I sit back down.

Seeing Mount Fuji has broken the ice on the train. There is a murmur of friendly voices the rest of the trip. Two hours after leaving Nagoya, we pull into Tokyo station. Anticipation bubbles through me. Tokyo, here I come!

We drop our bags at our hotel and then hit the subway. There are two maps of the subway on the wall. One has Japanese place names and one has English. The English doesn't help. The map is a total maze of colored lines.

"We're going to Ueno Park," Mr. Akimoto says, pointing toward the top of the English map.

"Now remember," Ms. Delucci warns. "We have to stick together. If anyone gets separated from the group, find a subway attendant. Ask them to page Mr. Akimoto, and then stay put."

With a little luck, maybe we'll lose Melissa and her groupies.

I half expect to see crowds of people being packed into subway cars by uniformed workers. I saw a clip of this on TV once. The workers were squeezing people in using something like push brooms. But it is not that bad now.

We finally emerge at Ueno Park. Unfortunately we haven't lost anyone. It's sunny out now. The wide sidewalk at the entrance to the park is lined with vendors selling food and souvenirs. Colorful banners with Japanese writing hang from many of the stalls.

Before Ms. Delucci has finished counting heads, DJ has bought a paper cone full of grilled meat. Melissa and a bunch of the girls are begging Mr. Crawford to let them get something before they faint from hunger. I can see that he is going to give in, so I head over to a stall selling shaved ice. I point to the red flavored syrup and hope for the best.

It turns out to be cherry and delicious.

Once everyone has food, we walk along the tree-lined sidewalk into the park. It's obviously a popular place. There are people everywhere—babies in strollers, gray-haired grandparents. There are groups of picnickers sitting on plastic blankets. I even see a few people dressed in kimonos.

In the trees overhead, huge crows caw loudly. One swoops down in front of us to snatch food from the sidewalk. Melissa squeals, and Zach lunges at the crow to scare it away. It flies up to a low tree branch and squawks at Zach and Melissa. Everyone else laughs. Several more crows join the first one. They caw at us as we pass under the tree.

"The Tokyo National Museum is just ahead," Mr. Crawford tells us, raising his voice. "We'll use the fountain in front of the museum as our meeting spot."

"Do we have to go *into* the museum?" someone asks.

Mr. Crawford narrows his eyes.

"Yes," he says. "This is a socials studies trip. I expect you to find at least two things in the museum to tell me about later."

Everyone groans.

The museum is an older, creamy-colored, stone building. In front of the entrance is a long rectangular pond with a low round fountain in the center.

We make arrangements to meet by the pond in two hours.

"And remember," Mr. Crawford says, "I expect each of you to tell me about two things you learn about in there."

With a group sigh, we head inside.

"He didn't say how long we have to stay," I hear DJ whisper. "We look at two things; then we're out of there."

chapter eleven

The first room of the museum is filled with old stone statues. They remind me of the statue with the bib in Seki-cho. Everyone from our group crowds around the statues. I guess we all had the same idea as DJ. Now I'll have to look at more things. I don't want to report to Mr. Crawford with the same thing as everyone else. I also don't want to leave the museum at the same time as the others.

I cut through the statue room and then through a room filled with samurai swords. The walls of the next room are hung with painted screens and scrolls—all behind glass. I take my time walking through this one. Colorful paintings of birds, trees and women wearing kimonos are all done using simple lines. They are kind of like manga, but with a different subject and style.

"You could do stuff like that," says a voice beside me.

I turn, startled. It's Zach.

"I looked at your sketchbook," he says. "You're pretty good."

"Thanks," I say warily. I search his face to see if he is making fun of me.

"Zach! What are you talking to *her* for?" Melissa's voice pierces the quiet. She stomps up and grabs Zach's arm. "Come on, we've seen more than two things. I want to get out of this boring hole."

Zach lets her drag him away, but he looks back at the museum cases as if he'd rather see more.

I continue making my way through the museum, stopping to look at things here and there. Many of the paintings, kimonos and tea bowls are hundreds of years old. Some of the statues and pottery are even a thousand years old. Pretty amazing.

When I leave the building, there is no one from my group in sight. I let out a deep satisfied sigh. Finally I am by myself.

Now that I've seen all the old art, I'd really like to see some new art. I wish I could visit a manga studio or see what kind of manga is for sale here. Maybe if I get out of the park I can find a store.

I take the path back toward the subway. The air is warm and slightly muggy. I look around as I walk, enjoying my freedom. With the Melly Mob out of the way, I can relax.

The area around the subway is crowded with small stores and restaurants, though there are no tall flashy buildings like we saw on the way to our hotel. I walk through the throng of people, pretending

I know where I'm going. Occasionally my red hair catches someone's attention and their eyes flick my way. But there are no rude stares.

There are stores selling stuff you might see anywhere—clothing, kitchenware, knick-knacks. Eventually I come to a convenience store. Through the window I see a long shelf of magazines, books and manga. A recorded female voice greets me as I walk through the door.

I pass shelves of intriguing-looking candy as I make my way to the books. The manga are piled on a lower shelf, beneath the magazines. The artwork on the covers immediately draws me in. There is boys' manga, girls' manga, kids' manga, adult manga. There's even X-rated manga sealed in plastic wrap. There are boys playing basketball, samurai warriors in sword fights and lovers about to kiss. There are ultramodern city settings and ancient Japanese village settings...

I flip through book after book. I am fascinated with the images. Though for the most part, I can't figure out what is happening.

After a while I pick out a couple of manga that I hope Fumiko and Kenji will like. I choose one for myself that has a style I want to study. Then I buy a bag of tiny moon-shaped crackers and some candy that has manga-style pictures of animals on the package. As I leave the store, the recorded voice thanks me.

Outside on the street, I start heading back toward the park. Or at least, that's what I think I'm doing. After a few blocks of walking, I stop and look around. Nothing looks familiar. The store beside me has a large red sign with black Japanese writing. Did I pass that sign before? I'm not sure. I walk a little farther. There's no sign of the park. A small tickle of panic stirs in the back of my chest.

I scan the faces of the people passing by. Do any of them speak English?

"Excuse me." I approach a middle-aged woman with a kind face. "Can you tell me the way to..."

She shakes her head and walks away before I can finish.

I look around again. Maybe someone younger would be more likely to speak English. I catch a young man's eye and step forward.

"Excuse me," I try again.

"Sorry," the man says. He looks a bit embarrassed. "My English not good." He starts to move away.

"Wait!" I call, grabbing hold of his arm.

He looks alarmed.

"Sorry." I let go quickly. I widen my eyes and attempt to give him a lost-puppy look. I hope my growing panic does not add a crazed tinge. I try to think of the simplest way to form my question.

"Can you tell me where Ueno Park is?" I ask.

He starts to shake his head.

"Ueno Park?" I ask again.

I can almost see the lightbulb turn on above his head.

"Ah, Ueno Park," he repeats, smiling.

He points using all his fingers, not just one. "Ueno Park that way," he says.

It's the opposite direction from the one I've been walking.

"Thank you! *Arigato gozaimsu*!" I tell him, not minding the looks my raised voice draws.

Relieved, I retrace my steps. It must be getting close to the time we're supposed to meet.

Finally I reach a park entrance. But it isn't the same one that I left earlier. A sign says *Ueno Park,* though. At least I know I'm in the right place. How hard can it be to find the museum?

I follow the path into the park. I watch for the stands where we bought food, the trees where we saw the crows or anything that looks familiar. I'd even be happy to see someone from my group.

"*Gaijin*," I hear a little girl say to her mom as they walk by. The mother shushes the girl and hurries her along.

Gaijin. Foreigner. Outsider.

I stop in the middle of the sidewalk

while people walk around me. Here I am, surrounded by people, and I feel more alone than I've ever felt before.

An older Japanese man approaches me and says something in Japanese. I can't tell if he's asking if I need help or if he's mad at me for blocking the sidewalk. I give him an apologetic shrug, turn and walk again.

There's got to be a sign with some directions around here somewhere. As I walk under the green trees, I hear crows call. The sidewalk leads to a hill covered with trees and then it forks to the left. There is a narrow stone path going up the hill. I leave the sidewalk and take the path. Maybe I'll be able to see the museum from the top of the hill.

As I climb, it's cooler under the trees. At first I hear the chirps of small birds, but then they are drowned by loud caws. The crows sound angry.

Someone screams.

I run along the path and stop at the top of the hill. Forgetting about the museum,

I scan the steps going down the other side of the hill. I can hardly believe what I see.

A few feet in front of me, Melissa and Zach duck their heads as two large crows dive-bomb them from the trees. One swoops within inches of Melissa's head. She swings her purse at it.

"Get away you stupid bird!" she screams.

At the sight of Zach and Melissa, relief bubbles through me. I quickly push it aside. Me, happy to see them? Not likely.

A second crow dives at Zach. He pulls up the collar of his T-shirt like a turtle trying to pull its head inside its shell.

They both look hilarious. I burst out laughing. That's when Melissa catches sight of me.

"You shut up!" she screeches, a look of pure hate on her face. Then she bursts into tears and runs down the stairs.

chapter twelve

Zach follows Melissa. The crows fly to a tree branch and continue cawing.

I walk carefully down the path, keeping one eye on the crows. They squawk at me but let me pass. In the branches above them I see what might be a nest.

I catch up to Zach and Melissa at the bottom of the hill. Melissa is sitting on a bench, her face in her hands. Zach reaches out to pat her.

I should find this scene entertaining. It is totally poetic justice that Melissa was attacked by a mob of crows. But her crying is taking the fun out of it.

I'd like to walk away, but I need directions back to the museum. Maybe I should just hide where I can see them and then follow them. Before I can make a move, Zach looks up and raises his hands in surrender.

"I don't know what to do," he says. "Everything is going wrong today...Can you tell us the way back to the museum?"

I stare at him for a few seconds.

"Come on," he says. "I don't know what the big fight is between you and Melissa, but can't you drop it for one day?"

By now Melissa has stopped crying and has turned away from us.

"Give it up, Zach," she grumbles. "She's not going to help us."

"She's not gonna just leave us here, Mel," says Zach.

"Oh? Why are you suddenly such an expert on Dana Edwards?" Melissa whirls around, her smudged mascara looks like war paint. She stares from Zach to me, her eyes accusing.

I remember the look she gave me when Zach talked to me at the stencil museum and how she pulled him away earlier today.

"You can't possibly think Zach and I are having some kind of affair!" I say, snorting with laughter.

"God!" Zach sputters in protest.

"Why not?" she says. "I'm sure you're more fun to be with on this trip than I am."

Whoa! That's about the last thing I expected to come out of her mouth.

"What are you talking about?" I say.

She starts crying again and throws up her hands.

"I hate it here!" she wails. "I just want to go home. I only came on the trip because Zach was going. I hate Japanese food! I hate being surrounded by people I can't understand! I hate the toilets! I never know the right thing to do...And you do everything right!"

Zach and I look at each other. He gives

me a shrug and walks away a few steps. Somehow this has become all about me and Melissa. I sit down on the bench beside her.

"What do you mean?" I ask. "I thought you hated everything I do."

"Nothing bothers you," she says. "You *do* weird. I can't."

"Thanks," I say sarcastically.

"Nothing scares you," she says.

I assume by this she is admitting that things *do* scare her. I sneak a look at her face. Underneath the red eyes and tear-streaked makeup, I glimpse the Melissa I used to know. Part of me wants to respond in the old way and offer sympathy. I take a deep breath and look up at the trees where the crows have now settled. All their bluster is really to protect their nest. Maybe Melissa's makeup and attitude is a form of protection. I remember how nervous she was about starting high school. She totally changed when we got there. She started wearing lots of makeup and trying to be Miss Popular. Was that how she dealt with being scared?

But then anger rises in me. Poor little frightened Melly. That doesn't explain why she started being such a jerk to me.

"You're so full of it, Mel," I snap. "You don't even *try* to like anything new. You act like everything different is crap and you're better than everyone else."

She gives me a disgusted look.

"Look who's talking," she sneers. "You're the stuck-up queen."

My mouth drops open. "What!? No way am I stuck-up!"

"Well, you could have fooled me!"

Zach takes a few steps toward us like he expects that we'll be going for each other's hair at any moment.

"Maybe you're not stuck-up," Melissa adds in a quieter tone. "But you act like you hate everyone."

She looks away when she says this. There is something odd in her voice—bitterness...or maybe hurt. It touches a raw place inside me. I'm tired of this pointless argument.

"Think that if you want!" I say, turning my back on her.

"See," she says. "That's just my point. You block everyone out. You act like you don't care about anything. Ever since we started high school you act like you don't even want people to like you. Like you're hiding behind some tough shell."

Tough shell. Fumiko told me I was like Kenji—hard on the outside. I slump back onto the bench and face her again.

"So, it's my fault that you and your friends treat me like pond scum. And if I'd just be nicer to you," I make my voice sarcastically sweet, "you'd be nicer to me."

She shrugs. "Something like that."

"And if you'd been nicer to me when we started high school, instead of ditching me to hang out with your new friends," I continue in the same sugary voice, "I wouldn't have acted like I hated you."

"Maybe," she says.

Suddenly I feel tired. Has my hating her been an act? Did she really think that I cut her out first?

chapter thirteen

"Hey, so if you're not going to kill each other..." Zach looks at his watch. "We should find our way back to the museum."

"Ah, about that...," I say as Melissa and I get to our feet. "I don't exactly know the way, either."

"You mean you're lost too?" Melissa whines. For a second, I think she's going to cry again. But then she laughs.

"Good," she says. "Because I really hated having to ask you for help."

"Me too." I grin at her like we're sharing

a joke. It's weird. Nothing has been resolved. But something has changed. Like the way the air smells after a storm.

Zach looks at us blankly, and then he throws up his hands.

"I give up. If you two want to stay lost, fine. But I'm going to go look for a sign or something."

He starts striding away from us. Melissa and I hurry to catch up.

"Look, there's a sign." Zach points to a spot where several pathways join.

It takes awhile to figure out the sign, but finally we agree on which way to go. By the time we make it back to the museum, everyone is waiting for us.

"What were you doing with *her*?" one of Melissa's friends hisses.

"Learning Japanese," Melissa says. "What do you think?"

I smile. Melissa and I may never be friends again, but maybe she isn't so bad.

In my hotel bed that night, I have a chance to think. Maybe we all have different ways of protecting ourselves. Melissa has her makeup and her attitude. DJ has his stupid humor, Fumiko has her cute things. I told myself I didn't care when Melissa and I stopped being friends. Told myself I didn't need anyone. Lying to yourself can be a way of protecting too.

The rest of the Tokyo trip goes too quickly: shopping on Omotesando and Harajuku streets where my unique fashion sense fits right in, playing games at Sega World. I even surprise myself and everyone else by challenging DJ to a game (which I win). We get to try karoke in our own private room on the last night.

When we board the train back to Suzuka there is a different feeling in the group. It's like we are an actual group, not just a bunch of people who don't like each other. I'm not saying I suddenly like everyone, but something has changed.

"Hey, Red!" DJ says, ruffling my hair.

"Hey, loser!" I say back, reaching out to flick the top of his head.

"Wait till next time, Red," he says.

"Yeah, right!" I laugh back. "You're a sucker for punishment."

As the train leaves Tokyo, I settle into my seat and take out my sketchbook. I stare at the unfinished manga girl. Something feels even less right about her now...Maybe she needs a sidekick or some kind of sword-wielding backup...I'm still trying to decide how to fix her when a new idea hits me. With a feeling of excitement, I flip to a fresh page and begin to draw.

About four hours later, we are back in Suzuka. Fumiko and her father meet me at the station. I'm glad to see them. In the van on the way to the Setos' house, I give Fumiko the manga book I bought for her and the drawing I did for her on the train. It's a manga-style version of Fumiko. She is standing between a Japanese woman in a kimono and a North American man in a business suit. They both look at Fumiko with expressions of sudden understanding on their faces. In a thought bubble above the woman's head is the Japanese word *hai*.

In a bubble above the man's head is the English word *yes*. Underneath the drawing I've written, *Fumiko Seto, #1 translator*.

"You drew me?" Fumiko asks, sounding amazed and pleased. "It is so good!"

After supper with the Setos, I give Kenji the book I picked out for him and another drawing I did on the train. This one is a manga version of Kenji playing soccer and scoring a goal. On the bottom of the drawing are the words, *Kenji Seto, soccer hero*.

I watch Kenji's face as he looks over the drawing, and I feel uncertain. Maybe I overdid it. I can see his lips mouth the words, "soccer hero." He probably thinks it's totally stupid.

But then Kenji looks up, grinning. It's the first real smile he's given me.

"Thank you," he says, his face red. He looks away and starts to leave, and then he turns back and gives me another smile.

chapter fourteen

We spend more time at the school during our last week. We even clean our classroom, which is a job students do in Japanese schools. It's supposed to develop team spirit and responsibility. I guess it works. Fumiko and the others seem happy to do most of the cleaning. With DJ joking around and Melissa and her friends whining, the Canadian group doesn't get much done.

We also spend more time with our host families. The Setos take me to one of

Kenji's soccer games. I actually have fun joining Fumiko in cheering and clapping. More people come out to watch than they do at our high school games. The cheers are also more polite—no *boos* or negative comments.

On the last day we visit Ise Shrine, an hour outside of Suzuka. The shrine is one of Japan's most famous, built in honor of the sun goddess. It's been in the same spot for almost two thousand years. We follow the path through a sacred forest that people have walked for centuries. When we get to the shrine, Fumiko and her family stop and say a prayer. Fumiko tells me that the shrine is rebuilt every twenty years.

"My parents helped pull the logs to the building site the last time," Fumiko says. "Next time Kenji and I will help."

"Don't they use trucks?" I ask.

"No," she explains. "Many people help float the logs down the river; then they use ropes to pull them up the path. It's been done that way for over a thousand years."

"Wow," I say. It's hard to imagine being part of something that old.

On my last night in Japan, Fumiko and I stand across the street from their house, looking out over the rice paddy. The plants have grown since I arrived. I feel like I know a lot more about Japan now but have still just touched the surface.

There's a sound from the house. We turn to see Kenji walking toward us.

"This is for you," he says carefully as he hands me a piece of paper.

"Thanks," I say, my curiosity rising.

Kenji points to the logo on his soccer jersey.

"I asked my teachers," he says.

I unfold the paper and read the neatly printed words, imagining the time it must have taken Kenji to get the English right.

An old Japanese story tells that long ago a monster was going to eat the sun. The rulers of heaven created the crow. The crow flew into the monster's mouth and choked it. Now the crow lives in the sun. It has three legs. One leg for dawn, one leg for noon and one leg for dusk. Another old story says that long ago the first emperor of Japan was traveling through the mountains and became lost. The sun goddess sent the crow with three legs to help him find the way home.

I think about the crows in Ueno Park. They helped me find my way in more ways than one. I wonder if one of them had three legs.

"This is interesting," I tell Kenji. He looks relieved. "So now the three-legged crow helps the Japanese soccer team?" I add.

It takes him a second to process what I've said. Then he nods and laughs. In the rice field, the frogs begin croaking.

"I still haven't seen a frog," I say.

"There!" Kenji says, pointing down at the water near our feet.

We lean forward, and this time I see it—a small green frog. It's visible for a second and then it disappears under the water.

"The Japanese word for frog, *kaeru*, sounds like the Japanese word for return home," Fumiko points out. "So the frog is a symbol for a safe return home."

Home. The three of us are quiet as we look out over the rice field. I think about the past three weeks. I can't remember what I expected, but I've learned that Japan is a place of old and new, side by side. A place where being part of a group is a good thing. And I've learned about myself.

I'm even looking forward to going home now, I realize. I'm looking forward to showing Fumiko around Vancouver when her group comes to Canada next month. Too bad Kenji isn't coming too.

"Let's not say good-bye," Fumiko says as if reading my thoughts. "Let's say *matta ne*. It means, See you again."

Matta ne, I promise silently. As we walk back to the house I realize I may still be a *gaijin*, but I no longer feel like a total outsider. And, I still have time for one last hot, relaxing, Japanese bath.

While researching *Manga Touch,* Jaqueline Pearce visited Japan and, like her main character Dana, she explored ancient sites as well as modern Tokyo. During the writing of the book at her home in Vancouver, British Columbia, she continued to immerse herself in Japanese culture, from history and myths to anime, manga and food. Jaqueline is the author of several books for children, including *Dog House Blues* and *The Truth about Rats and Dogs.*

Orca Currents

Visit www.orcabook.com for all Orca titles.